AMERICAN INDIAN
PRA...
&
Poetry

Designed & Edited by
J. Ed Sharpe

Illustrated by
William Taylor

CHEROKEE PUBLICATIONS
P.O. BOX 256

PREFACE

Prayers and Poetry of all peoples of all times carry man's religious symbols in their purest and most beautiful form.

These symbols jump like mountain wildfire from people to people, from age to age, from religion to religion, and in so jumping they bridge the gaps of differences in our beliefs and illuminate the universal oneness of us all.

The American Indian has had a way of expressing these symbols in vivid and poetic ways, thereby weaving his basic beliefs into a spiritual rug of infinite color and pattern with the beliefs of all.

The American Indian used earth symbols such as the eagle, the fish, light, rain, shadow, wind, grass, water, sun, stars, fire, smoke, valleys and hills. We all readily identify with these, because being on the earth, they are not of the earth, but rather are carrier words for infinite and universal truths.

The expressions included here span centuries of time from ancient inscriptions to recent and modern day writings; yet they have a unity that bespeaks their ageless character. Perhaps they will awaken or sharpen the awareness of the reader to spiritual realities of our time. If so, my collection and assemblage has been of value.

— *ED SHARPE*

MY FACE

My face is a mask I order to say
nothing
About the fragile feelings hiding in my
soul.

— Glenn Lazore
(Mohawk)

Look to this day,
For yesterday is already a dream
And tomorrow only a vision
But today
Well lived, makes every
Yesterday a dream of
Happiness and every tomorrow
A vision of hope.
Look well
Therefore to
This day.

—Author Unknown

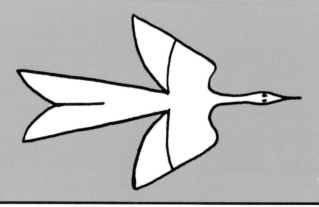

COME ON THE TRAIL OF SONG

Come on the trail of song,
Leaving no footprints there,
Over the rainbow bridge
Down the mountain stair.

Come on the trail of song,
Gods of the Navajo,
Out of the sky-land
And the five worlds below.

—Eda Lou Walton

CHINOOK LORD'S PRAYER

Nesika papa klaksta mitlite kopa saghalie
  Our Father Who dwells on High

Kloshe kopa nesika tumtum mika nem.
  Good for our hearts Your Name.

Kloske mika tyee kopa konaway tillikum;
  Good you Chief of all people;

Kloshe mika tumtum kopa illahee kahkwa kopa saghalie;
  Good Your heart to make our country such as Yours
  up above;

Potlatch konaway sun nesika muckamuck,
  Give us all days our food,

Pee kopet-kumtux donaway nesika mesachie,
  And stop remembering all our sins we make to them,

Kahkwa nesilka mamook kopa klasksta spose mamook
mesachie kopa nesia;
  As we suppose not their sin against us;

Mahah siah kopa nesika konaway mesachie.
  Throw far away from us all evil.

              Kloshe kahkwa.
              Amen.

When you arise in the morning,
give thanks for the morning light,
for your life and strength.
give thanks for your food
and the joy of living.

If you see no reason for giving thanks,
the fault lies in yourself.

—Tecumseh

THE LIGHTS

The Sun is a luminous shield
Borne up the blue path
By a god;

The moon is the torch
Of an old man
Who stumbles over the stars.

—Eda Lou Walton

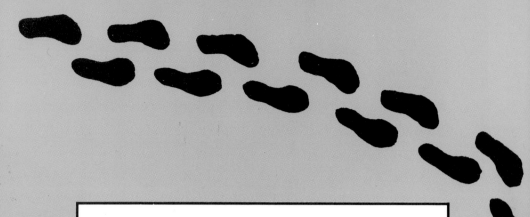

SUN TRACKS

the Track of the Sun
across the Sky
leaves its shining message,
Illuminating,
Strengthening,
Warming,
us who are here,
showing us we are not alone,
we are yet ALIVE!
And this fire . . .
Our fire...
Shall not die!

—Atoni
(Choctaw)

CHEROKEE PRAYER

As I walk the trail of life
in the fear of the wind and
rain,
grant O Great Spirit
that I may always walk
like a man.

THE SIOUX AT PRAYER

As quietly as little rabbit's feet,
The morning glory sun arrives to greet
The Red Man as he worships in his way.
For this he asks the Spirit every day;
"Before I judge my friend, O let me wear
His moccasins for two long weeks, and share
The path that he would take in wearing them;
Then, I shall understand and not condemn.

—Peggy Windsor Garnett

YOU ARE PART OF ME

You are part of me now
* You touched me.*
With your kindness and love
* So enchanted.*
Your soft lips are kind.
* Your eyes glow with life.*
I'm glad you touched me.
* You're part of me now.*

—Lloyd Carl Owle
*   (Cherokee)*

MOHAWK INDIAN PRAYER

Oh Great Spirit, Creator of all things;
Human Beings, trees, grass, berries.
Help us, be kind to us.
Let us be happy on earth.
Let us lead our children
To a good life and old age.
These our people; give them good minds
To love one another.
Oh Great Spirit,
Be kind to us.
Give these people the favour
To see green trees,
Green grass, flowers, and berries
This next spring;
So we all meet again.
Oh Great Spirit,
We ask of you.

—Author Unknown

OJIBWA PRAYER

Oh Great Spirit, whose voice I hear in the winds
And whose breath gives life to everyone,
Hear me.
I come to you as one of your many children;
I am weak . . . I am small . . . I need your wisdom
  and your strength.
Let me walk in beauty, and make my eyes ever
  behold the red and purple sunsets.
Make my hands respect the things you have made,
  and make my ears sharp so I may hear your
voice.
Make me wise, so that I may understand what you
  have taught my people and
The lessons you have hidden in each leaf
  and each rock.
I ask for wisdom and strength,
Not to be superior to my brothers, but to be able
  to fight my greatest enemy, myself.
Make me ever ready to come before you with
  clean hands and a straight eye,
So as life fades away as a fading sunset,
My spirit may come to you without shame.

—Author Unknown

INDIAN PRAYER

Oh our Mother the earth, Oh our Father the sky,
Your children are we, and with tired backs
We bring you the gifts you love.

Then weave for us a garment of brightness;

May the Warp be the white light of morning,
May the weft be the red light of evening,
May the fringes be the falling rain,
May the border be the standing rainbow.

Thus weave for us a garment of brightness,
That we may walk fittingly where birds sing,
That we may walk fittingly where grass is green,

Oh our Mother earth, Oh our Father sky.

THE HUNTERS

There were but two beneath the sky -
The thing I came to kill, and I.
I, under covert, quietly
Watched him sense eternity
From quivering brush to pointed nose
My gun to shoulder level rose.
And then I felt (I could not see)
Far off a hunter watching me.
I slowly put my rifle by,
For there were two who had to die -
The thing I wished to kill, and I.

—Author Unknown

THE
TWENTY THIRD PSALM

(AN INDIAN VERSION)

The GREAT FATHER above a SHEPHERD CHIEF is.
I am His and with Him I want not.
He throws out to me a rope
and the name of the rope is love
and He draws me to where the grass is green
and the water is not dangerous,
and I eat and lie down and am satisfied.
Sometimes my heart is very weak and falls down
but He lifts me up again and draws me into a good road.
His name is WONDERFUL.

Sometime, it may be very soon, it may be a long long time,
He will draw me into a valley.
It is dark there, but I'll be afraid not,
for it is between those mountains
that the SHEPHERD CHIEF will meet me
and the hunger that I have in my heart all through life
will be satisfied.

Sometimes he makes the love rope into a whip,
but afterwards He gives me a staff to lean upon.
He spreads a table before me with all kinds of foods.
He puts His hand upon my head and all the "tired" is gone.
My cup he fills till it runs over.
What I tell is true.
I lie not.
These roads that are "away ahead" will stay with me
through this life and after;
and afterwards I will go to live in the Big Teepee
and sit down with the SHEPHERD CHIEF forever.

—George Hunt
(Kiowa)

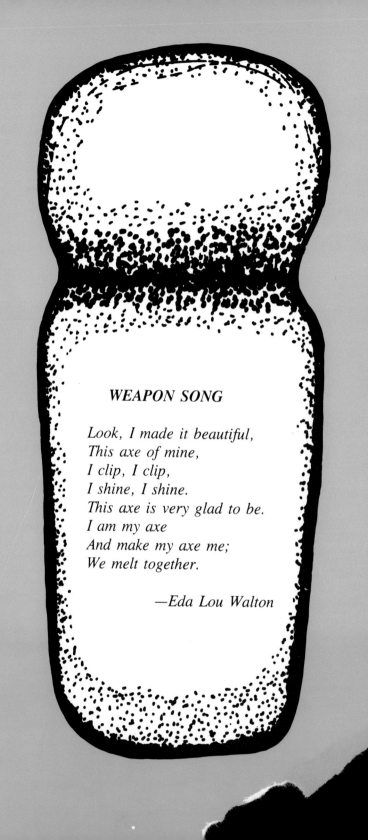

WEAPON SONG

Look, I made it beautiful,
This axe of mine,
I clip, I clip,
I shine, I shine.
This axe is very glad to be.
I am my axe
And make my axe me;
We melt together.

—Eda Lou Walton

GIFTS OF THE GODS

They have given me of soft goods,
Good and beautiful skins and furs,
And of hard goods, beads and haliotis shells,
Of many domestic animals
And of animals to hunt,
Corn of the rainbow color,
Black clouds, mists, male-rains
And the soft gray female-rain,
Lightning, plants, and pollen
For my voice, my limbs, my mind;
I am beautiful
In gratitude.

—Eda Lou Walton

REMNANTS

Deserted towers and sacred kivas
Built in cliffs beneath the sky,
Mere remnants of an ancient culture
In desolated ruins lie.

Petroglyphs with secret message
Modern age cannot unfold . . .
Strange, unique, mysterious carvings
Of tribal legends yet untold.

Why went this race and left none after
In sunbaked homes of earthen floor?
Rain tower, watchtower, both deserted,
Nothing now but Indian lore.

—Viva Sue Lett

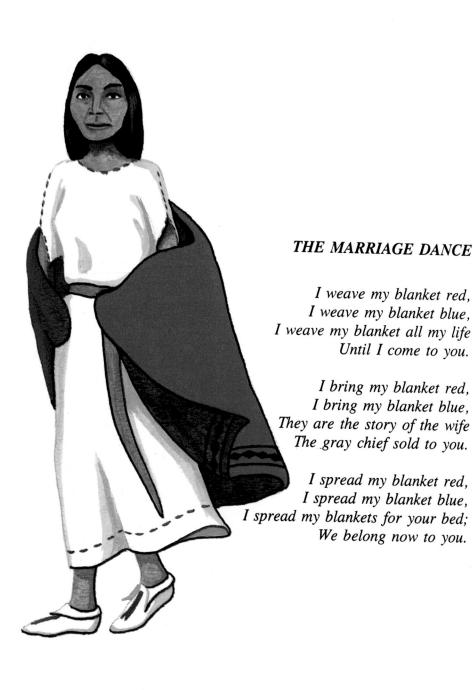

THE MARRIAGE DANCE

I weave my blanket red,
I weave my blanket blue,
I weave my blanket all my life
Until I come to you.

I bring my blanket red,
I bring my blanket blue,
They are the story of the wife
The gray chief sold to you.

I spread my blanket red,
I spread my blanket blue,
I spread my blankets for your bed;
We belong now to you.

THE MOCCASINS OF AN OLD MAN

I hung you there, moccasins of worn buckskin.
I hung you there and there you are still.
I took you from the hot flesh of a swift buck.
I took you to my woman.

She tanned you with buck brains.
She cut and sewed and beaded.
I wore you with pride.
I wore you with leaping steps over many grounds.

Now, I sit here and my bones
are stiff with many winters.
You hang there and I shall sit.
We shall watch the night
approach.

—Romona Carden
(Colville)

VOICES THAT BEAUTIFY THE EARTH

Voice above,
Voice of Thunder,
Speak from the dark of clouds;
Voice below,
Grasshopper-voice,
Speak from the green of plants;
So may the earth be beautiful.

DAYBREAK SONG

All night the gods were with us,
Now night is gone;
Silence the rattle,
Sing the daybreak song,
For in the dawn Bluebird calls,
And out from his blankets of tumbled gray
The Sun comes, combing his hair for the day.

PRAYER FOR THE HARVEST

I enter into the House of the Red Rock
Made holy by visiting gods,
And into the House of Blue Water
I am come.
Enter me, Spirit of my forgotten Grandmother,
That curtains of rain may hang
All dark before me,
That tall corn may shake itself
Above my head.

—Eda Lou Walton

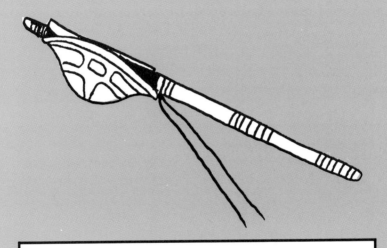

MAY THE GREAT SPIRIT
WATCH OVER YOU

AS LONG AS THE
GRASS GROWS AND
THE WATER FLOWS

TEARS

Not in the time of pleasure
Hope doth set her bow;
But in the sky of sorrow,
Over the vale of woe.

Through gloom and shadow look we
On beyond the years:
The soul would have no rainbow
Had the eyes no tears.

—John Vance Chenay

THE ROCK

The rock lays near
  While light comes and goes
  The rock only exists
    Said to have no soul
      The rock cannot be sad
        It knows not the time
          It has no life to hold
            It can't feel love
              As we admire it
                It remains in stillness
                  Yet in its own way
                    May watch!

—Lloyd Carl Owle
(Cherokee)

A PRAYER OF THE AMERICAN INDIAN

Oh Great Spirit

Let your voice whisper righteousness in our ear through the West Wind in the late of the day.

Let us be comforted with love for our brothers and sisters with no war.

Let us hold good health mentally and physically to solve our problems and accomplish something for future generations of life.

Let us be sincere to ourselves and our youth and make the world a better place to live.

—Lloyd Carl Owle
(Cherokee)

INDIAN PRAYER AT EVENING

One sunset hour
Wrapped in sacrificial fire
Then shall I enter Thee,
Spirit of all sands,
And Thy night
Will cool my small desire
to be among my kinsman.

—Eda Lou Walton

FINAL VISION

*Life is the flash
      of a firefly in the night.
It is the breath of a buffalo
      in the winter.
It is the little shadow
      which runs across the grass
      and loses itself
      in the sunset.*

— *Crowfoot,
      (Blackfoot)*

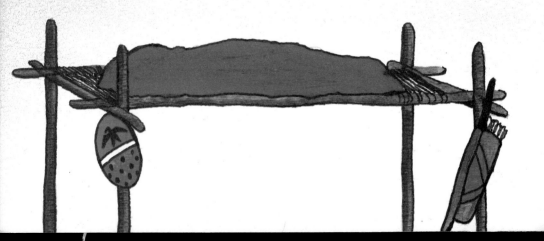

BLACK ELK'S PRAYER

Hey-a-a-hay! Lean to hear my feeble voice.
At the center of the sacred hoop
You have said that I should make the tree to
bloom.
With tears running, O Great Spirit, my
Grandfather,
With running eyes I must say
The tree has never bloomed
Here I stand, and the tree is withered.
Again, I recall the great vision you gave me.
It may be that some little root of the sacred tree
still lives.
Nourish it then
That it may leaf
And bloom
And fill with singing birds!
Hear me, that the people may once again go back
To the Sacred Hoop
Find the good road
And the shielding tree.

—Black Elk

OUR THANKS FOR THE USE OF MATERIAL GOES TO:

All authors whose names appear with their material.
All authors who were "unknown".

Sun Tracks Literary Quarterly, Copyright c 1971
"SUN TRACKS" Vol 1, #1, Summer 1971
Reprinted by special permission . . . "Sun Tracks"

American Indian Missions, Inc.
"An Indian Version Of The 23rd Psalm"

Akwesasne Notes, Early Autumn, 1971.
Mohawk Nation, via Rooseveltown, NY.
First appeared in Chemehuevi Newsletter, "Tears"

Haskell Institute Newsletter
"INDIAN LEADER" 11/15/68 for "Look To This Day"

E. P. Dutton & Co. NY
From book: DAWN BOY
    "Come On The Trail Of Song"
    "The Lights"
    "Weapon Song"
    "Gifts of the Gods"
    "Voices That Beautify The Earth"
    "Prayer For The Harvest"